Natural Laboratories:
Scientists in National Parks

ROCKY
MOUNTAIN

Christy Mihaly

Educational Media

rourkeeducationalmedia.com

Before, During, and After Reading Activities

Before Reading: Building Background Knowledge and Academic Vocabulary

"Before Reading" strategies activate prior knowledge and set a purpose for reading. Before reading a book, it is important to tap into what your child or students already know about the topic. This will help them develop their vocabulary and increase their reading comprehension.

Questions and activities to build background knowledge:
1. *Look at the cover of the book. What will this book be about?*
2. *What do you already know about the topic?*
3. *Let's study the Table of Contents. What will you learn about in the book's chapters?*
4. *What would you like to learn about this topic? Do you think you might learn about it from this book? Why or why not?*

Building Academic Vocabulary
Building academic vocabulary is critical to understanding subject content.
Assist your child or students to gain meaning of the following vocabulary words.
Content Area Vocabulary
Read the list. What do these words mean?

- adaptive
- civilizations
- climate
- compounds
- deposition
- exterminated
- fertilizer
- inventory
- microscopic
- policies
- sufficient
- tolerate

During Reading: Writing Component

"During Reading" strategies help to make connections, monitor understanding, generate questions, and stay focused.
1. *While reading, write in your reading journal any questions you have or anything you do not understand.*
2. *After completing each chapter, write a summary of the chapter in your reading journal.*
3. *While reading, make connections with the text and write them in your reading journal.*
   a) *Text to Self – What does this remind me of in my life? What were my feelings when I read this?*
   b) *Text to Text – What does this remind me of in another book I've read? How is this different from other books I've read?*
   c) *Text to World – What does this remind me of in the real world? Have I heard about this before? (News, current events, school, etc....)*

After Reading: Comprehension and Extension Activity

"After Reading" strategies provide an opportunity to summarize, question, reflect, discuss, and respond to text. After reading the book, work on the following questions with your child or students to check their level of reading comprehension and content mastery.
1. *What subjects have researchers studied at Rocky Mountain National Park? (Summarize)*
2. *How could scientists figure out where the excess nitrogen in Rocky Mountain National Park came from? (Infer)*
3. *What are some ways human actions have affected Rocky Mountain National Park? (Asking Questions)*
4. *If you joined a citizen science project in Rocky Mountain National Park, what work would you like to do? (Text to Self Connection)*

Extension Activity
Scientists use computer models to predict how changes in one part of an ecosystem can affect other aspects of the system. For example, if the elk herd increases to 1,500 animals, what will happen to the willows? If you were creating a model of the relationships between elk, willows, and beaver, what data would you need? What variables (elk population, acres of willow, etc.) might you include in the computer model?

TABLE OF CONTENTS

CHAPTER ONE

ELK AND ECOSYSTEMS

Snow-capped mountains, pine-covered slopes, and treeless tundra greet visitors to Rocky Mountain National Park (RMNP) in Colorado. The park's 415 square miles (1,075 square kilometers) are 95 percent wilderness. More than 100 of its mountain peaks stand more than 10,000 feet (3,048 meters) tall. Hikers can follow many miles of backcountry trails, while park roads allow drivers to enjoy scenery and wildlife from their cars.

The granite of RMNP's high peaks was formed more than one billion years ago. Geologists study the structure and content of these rocks to learn how Earth and its landscapes were formed.

High in the Rockies

Most of RMNP lies more than 9,000 feet (2,743 meters) above sea level. The park's highest point, Longs Peak, is 14,259 feet (4,346 meters) tall. Trail Ridge Road, North America's highest continuous paved highway, goes up to 12,183 feet (3,713 meters).

Trail Ridge Road running through RMNP

Each year, more than four million people visit RMNP. To preserve the park's natural resources the National Park Service depends on scientists. Biologists, ecologists, and other researchers study the park's ecosystems and the plants and animals living there—from elk in the highway to algae in mountain lakes. Their findings help form park **policies**.

Drivers and bikers must be on the lookout for elk.

green algae

lake in RMNP

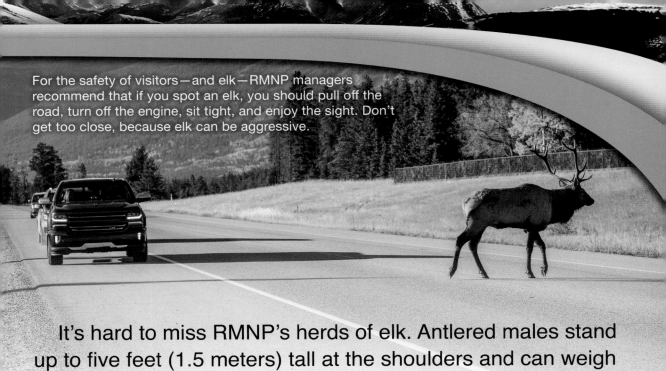

For the safety of visitors—and elk—RMNP managers recommend that if you spot an elk, you should pull off the road, turn off the engine, sit tight, and enjoy the sight. Don't get too close, because elk can be aggressive.

It's hard to miss RMNP's herds of elk. Antlered males stand up to five feet (1.5 meters) tall at the shoulders and can weigh more than 1,100 pounds (499 kilograms). Elk often graze by roadsides. Sometimes they stop in the middle of the road.

Male elk, called bulls, grow a new set of antlers each spring.

elk herd

Wapiti

Elk are also called wapiti. This word comes from the name for the animal in the Algonquian languages, a group of American Indian tongues. The Shawnee and Cree people called the

grizzly bear

Before the 20th century, predators such as the gray wolf and grizzly bear roamed this wilderness and fed on elk. But as settlers moved in, they wanted to protect their livestock. They **exterminated** most of these predators around RMNP. The elk population soared.

gray wolf

By the late 1990s, so many hungry elk were browsing the park's plants that they caused serious damage. Scientists found the park's willow and aspen trees were scarred and unable to produce new growth. They also determined that the numerous elk were outcompeting other species—there weren't enough willows for everyone.

The moose, another large RMNP mammal, also relies on willows as a food source.

large elk herd

elk in RMNP

Ecosystem Modeling

*In an ecosystem, the relationships between species are complex.
Scientists created computer models to help them analyze how
changes in elk management might affect the populations of
different species in the park.*

Scientists have fitted some female elk in RMNP with radio collars. These
help them track the elk and study their migration, health, and habitat use.

The beaver will slap its flat, scaly tail on the water to warn other beavers of danger.

Beavers, once common in the park, are now rarely seen there. Beavers rely on willows for food and also as material to build dams. Scientists estimate that a beaver colony requires about ten acres (four hectares) of tall willows to survive. Without **sufficient** willows, the beavers of RMNP died off.

That's bad news not only for beavers, but for other park residents too. Beavers dam streams to create ponds and wetlands, providing a valuable habitat for many animals and plants. With the beavers gone, conditions are drier.

dry Colorado creek bed

beaver dam and pond

Busy Beavers

Beavers are nature's engineers. A beaver family or several families living in a colony will build dams across streams to form beaver ponds. They construct their lodges in these ponds, putting entrances under the water for protection against predators.

elk fence

Volunteers help park rangers collect data on animals in RMNP.

Scientists concluded there were about 1,000 elk spending the winter in RMNP—more than the park could handle. Based on their findings, park managers developed solutions. In 2008, RMNP adopted a 20 year plan. It called for reducing the herd from 800 to 600, replanting trees, and fencing heavily browsed areas to exclude elk and allow plants to grow back.

The elk population has now decreased. The aspens have started to recover, and programs to restore willows are underway. Plan implementation includes ongoing monitoring of plants and animals. Park managers continually adjust their efforts based on new data, using a technique known as **adaptive** management.

Chronic Wasting Disease

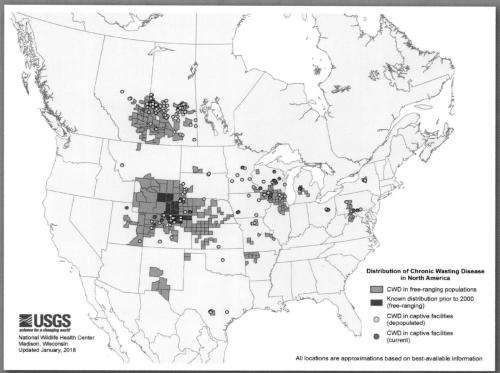

Chronic Wasting Disease

Some elk in RMNP are infected with Chronic Wasting Disease (CWD), a fatal illness affecting wild deer and elk. As part of ongoing herd management, researchers are evaluating the extent of CWD and its effect on the elk population.

CHAPTER TWO

NITROGEN IN WATER AND AIR

In 1982, ecologist Jill Baron started hauling scientific instruments to remote RMNP locations to analyze the water there. More than 35 years later, her team of scientists continues gathering data every week, collecting samples from mountain lakes and streams, measuring rainfall and snowfall, and monitoring the **microscopic** plants and animals—algae and plankton—in the water. This long-term data collection has been important in understanding the health of the park environment.

Scientists take to the field to monitor the snow depth and moisture content.

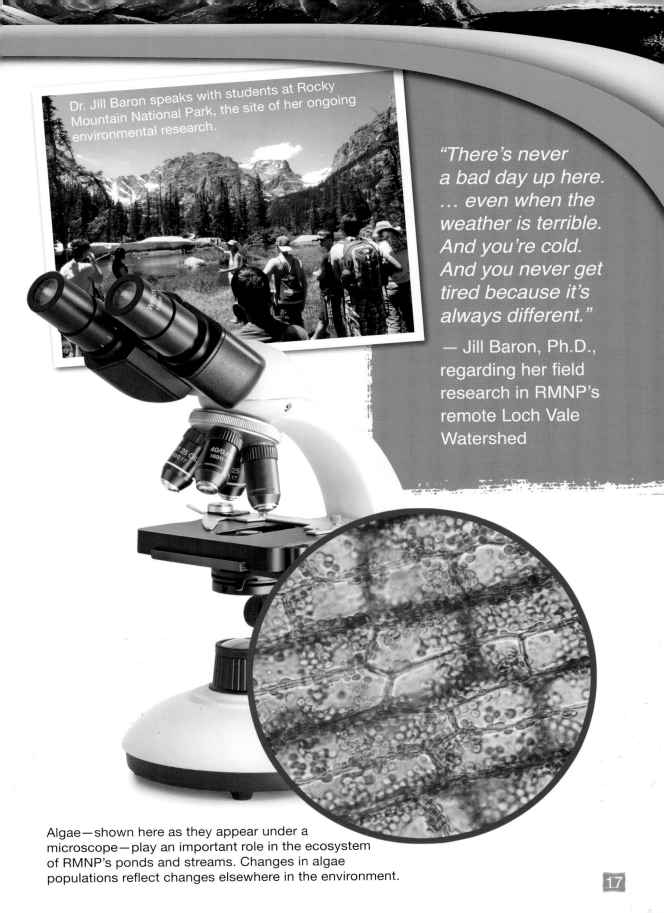

Dr. Jill Baron speaks with students at Rocky Mountain National Park, the site of her ongoing environmental research.

"There's never a bad day up here. ... even when the weather is terrible. And you're cold. And you never get tired because it's always different."

— Jill Baron, Ph.D., regarding her field research in RMNP's remote Loch Vale Watershed

Algae—shown here as they appear under a microscope—play an important role in the ecosystem of RMNP's ponds and streams. Changes in algae populations reflect changes elsewhere in the environment.

The samples from mountain lakes alerted scientists to high nitrogen levels in the water. Nitrogen is a natural element that is essential for plant and animal life. Its impacts in cities are not visible. But in delicate mountain environments, excess nitrogen acts as a **fertilizer** and throws the ecosystem out of balance.

7

N

Nitrogen

The element nitrogen, indicated by the symbol "N," is colorless and odorless in its gas form. Nitrogen makes up about 78 percent of the air around Earth.

Field scientists have built a large and valuable database by regularly collecting and analyzing samples from RMNP water bodies.

Remote mountain lakes in RMNP appear untouched by civilization, but water samples indicate they are affected by air pollution.

Fish kills, like the one pictured here, can result from high water acidity and low oxygen levels in the water.

Mountain lakes are naturally low in nitrogen. Too much nitrogen can alter algae and plankton growth in the lakes. It causes some species to grow faster and enables invasive species to thrive. Eventually, high nitrogen levels also make lake waters more acidic, which can cause fish to die.

Automobiles, like these driving on RMNP's Trail Ridge Road, are a major source of nitrogen oxide pollution in the air.

The excess nitrogen comes from air pollution. RMNP is near urban and industrial areas and large farms which emit compounds containing nitrogen into the air. These **compounds** include nitrogen oxides, from burning fossil fuels in vehicles and factories, and ammonia from animal waste and commercial fertilizers. The contaminants are carried into the park by falling rain and snow and blowing dust.

The growing town of Estes Park, Colorado, sits just outside the RMNP boundaries. To the east, larger cities including Boulder, Fort Collins, and Westminster lie within 50 miles (80 kilometers) of the park.

By testing nitrogen levels in soil, scientists are monitoring changes in the RMNP caused by airborne nitrogen from urban areas.

Nitrogen in the Soil

Researchers also documented high nitrogen levels in RMNP soil and plants. Experiments demonstrate that adding nitrogen changes the types of plants that grow in the park's meadows and forests.

This information led scientists and policy makers from RMNP, the State of Colorado, and the federal Environmental Protection Agency (EPA) to formulate measures for reducing nitrogen **deposition** in RMNP. In 2007, they jointly adopted a plan. Since then, emissions from vehicles and power plants have been reduced through regulations. Colorado agriculture organizations are working voluntarily to reduce ammonia releases.

A scientist collects water samples.

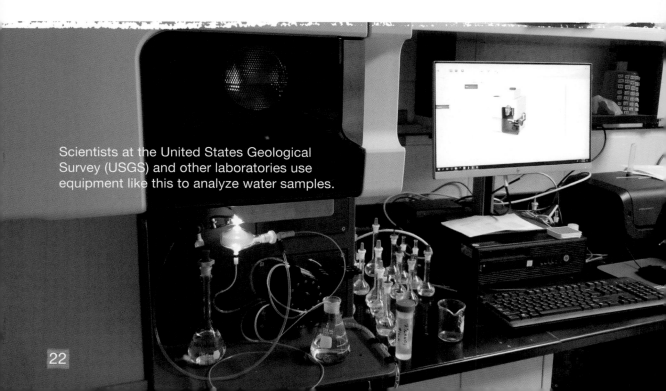
Scientists at the United States Geological Survey (USGS) and other laboratories use equipment like this to analyze water samples.

For example, farmers will avoid fertilizing fields during weather patterns when ammonia is more likely to be spread in the air.

By 2012, the deposition of nitrogen into RMNP had stopped increasing. Reducing it further will be difficult. In considering next steps, scientists and park managers must analyze the issue of nitrogen deposition in combination with other park changes including warmer, drier conditions.

Spraying fertilizers during low-wind conditions helps reduce the spread of

CHAPTER THREE

COPING WITH A CHANGING CLIMATE

Plants in RMNP must withstand cold temperatures and icy conditions.

Spring snowmelt swells the streams as the water runs down from the high mountains.

The plants and animals of RMNP have adapted to survive severe cold and snow. They face new challenges now, as the park's **climate** changes.

red fox

According to the National Park Service, the average annual temperature in RMNP has risen 3.4 degrees Fahrenheit (1.9 degrees Celsius) over the past century. And spring arrives earlier. Between 1978 and 2007, the annual snowmelt shifted about two to three weeks earlier. This means the melted snow flows out of RMNP earlier, leaving less water in park rivers during the summer. These changes have affected many plants and animals.

Black bears and other RMNP animals rely on water from snowmelt.

Spring brings rushing waters and blooming flowers to RMNP.

The American pika, a small mammal well-suited to survive in high, cold mountain habitats, may face extinction in RMNP. It cannot **tolerate** temperatures as high as 75 degrees Fahrenheit (24 degrees Celsius) for more than a few hours. As conditions warm, scientists are tracking the pikas' movement and health. The animals are relocating to higher, cooler elevations, and may become overcrowded or run out of food sources in the upper mountain reaches.

pika sitting in snow

Beetle-killed pine trees are a common sight in RMNP. Higher temperatures and lack of rain have weakened the trees, while allowing the beetles to thrive.

Pine showing internal destruction from the pine beetle.

pine beetle

Beetles Benefit from the Change

Some species benefit from warmer winters. For example, when there's no deep freeze, more mountain pine beetle larvae survive the winter. Beetle populations have recently soared in RMNP, resulting in heavy beetle infestations of the forests, and many dead trees.

During the winter, the white-tailed ptarmigan usually avoids flying to conserve its energy. It's barely visible against the snow.

The white-tailed ptarmigan is another RMNP inhabitant whose numbers have declined. This bird turns white in the winter for camouflage. Scientists are studying ptarmigans using tracking devices.

In its summer plumage, the white-tailed ptarmigan often moves to lower elevations where it seeks fruits, insects, and flowers to eat.

They have found that with warmer temperatures earlier in the spring, ptarmigans build nests and lay eggs earlier. One reason for the birds' decline may be that the eggs hatch before the plants that chicks feed on are blooming. More study is needed to understand what's happening with the ptarmigan population.

Researchers are also working to protect a less visible park inhabitant, the boreal toad. A decline in the toad's population, due in part to disease, has landed it on Colorado's endangered species list. Biologists believe the hotter, drier climate may make the toad more vulnerable to infection.

The toad disease chytridiomycosis is caused by a fungus, Batrachochytrium dendrobatidis (Bd). It interferes with the toads' ability to breathe and absorb water through their skin. Biologists are seeking ways to fight the infection.

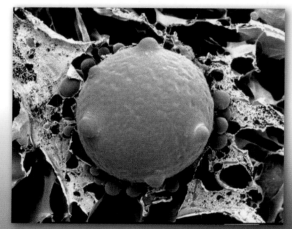

The chytrid fungus, captured in this image taken by a scanning electron microscope, causes fatal infections in many species of amphibians.

boreal toad on log

Amphibians infected with chytridiomycosis, like this frog, often die.

Frog Fungus

Amphibian chytridiomycosis has contributed to a steep decline in global populations of amphibians—toads, frogs, salamanders, and newts. It has spread to all continents except Antarctica and has been found in more than 100 species.

In addition, scientists have raised thousands of boreal toad tadpoles in offsite facilities. By releasing healthy tadpoles into RMNP, they hope to help the toad population recover there.

Scientists don't know how many of the captive-raised tadpoles are growing into adults. They hope to improve their understanding by marking and counting toads in the field.

A female boreal toad lays up to 16,000 eggs in shallow water.

CHAPTER FOUR

ARCHAEOLOGY IN THE ICE

Humans have been present in the Rocky Mountains for more than 10,000 years. One thousand years ago, Ute and other American Indian peoples hunted in what is now RMNP.

This 1890 oil painting portrays a bison hunt. Bison, although native to the area that is now RMNP, no longer live there.

Colorow, shown here, was one of the best-known leaders of the Ute people in Colorado in the nineteenth century. He saw many changes from the time white settlers first arrived through the removal of his people to a Utah reservation.

Archaeologists working in RMNP today search for signs of early humans. They have found objects left by ancient **civilizations** at more than 1,000 sites in the park. The evidence suggests that long ago, people traveled between cold season camps at lower altitudes and higher-altitude hunting camps in warmer weather, following the migration of elk and other game.

Louisiana Purchase

The Louisiana Purchase doubled the size of the United States, with the addition of 827,000 square miles (2.14 million square kilometers) of land.

Under the reservation system, the United States set aside certain lands for American Indians to live on as settlers moved in and took over their territories.

Displaced Peoples

In the 1803 Louisiana Purchase, the United States bought the territory including present-day Colorado from France. White European settlers poured in. In the 1870s, the United States government removed the Ute people from the area, sending them to reservations.

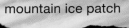

Archaeologists drill into the ice to take core samples. The sample can be analyzed to determine the age of the ice at various depths.

At most archaeological sites, digging reveals bones and objects made of durable materials such as stone. However, the warming conditions in RMNP have revealed new treasures under mountain ice. As long-frozen ice melts, it enables researchers to conduct "ice patch archaeology." Ice patches— large snowbanks that have been frozen for hundreds or thousands of years—preserve many objects such as wooden hunting tools, leather clothing, and baskets.

RMNP's Tyndall Glacier is a small cirque glacier, meaning it was created by the accumulation of snow and ice in a bowl-shaped depression in the side of the mountain.

Researchers in the snow and ice must be prepared for a range of working conditions.

Ice Patches versus Glaciers

A glacier is a mass of ice accumulated from compacted snow which flows slowly downhill—a river of ice. Smaller ice patches, in contrast, don't move. Scientists are studying whether RMNP's mountain glaciers are shrinking, like those in polar regions.

By investigating ice patches, scientists can also learn about the long-ago environment. At one RMNP site, they discovered a 4,000-year-old spruce log. The changing climate is offering scientists new information about the earth's past.

Core samples from ancient ice allow scientists to glimpse into the past. For example, by analyzing bubbles in the ice, scientists learn what gases were in the earth's atmosphere hundreds of thousands of years ago.

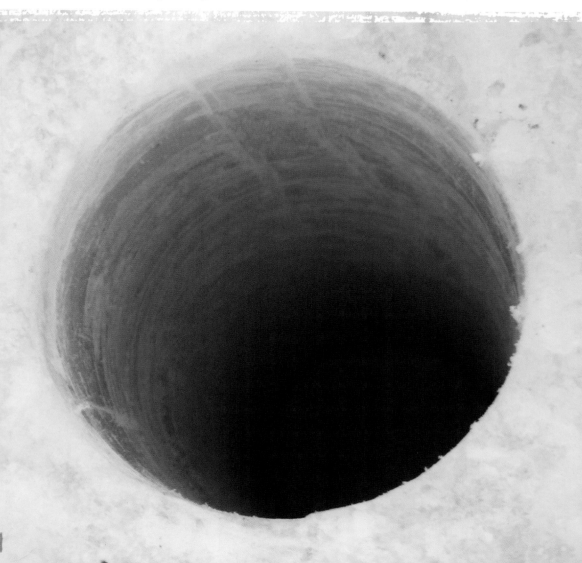

Archaeologists utilize a theodolite, an instrument that helps them map their location by measuring angles.

"What we're finding as archaeologists is stuff that was lost. … It's like finding your keys when you drop them in snow. You're not going to find them until spring. Well, the spring hasn't come until these things started melting for the first time, in some instances, in many, many thousands of years."

— Archaeologist Craig Lee, Ph.D., after discovering a 10,000-year-old wooden hunting tool in a melting ice patch

CHAPTER FIVE

CITIZEN SCIENTISTS MAKE A DIFFERENCE

It's not only professional scientists who conduct research in RMNP. Thousands of volunteers help. They hike into the park to take measurements, count plants and animals, and collect samples. Citizen scientists offer extra hands and eyes for researchers.

Taking a close look reveals the river is home to many species of plants and animals.

Being a citizen scientist can mean counting black flies.

BioBlitz volunteers work to complete their species counts.

National Park Service director Jonathan B. Jarvis speaks at BioBlitz.

Taking an **inventory** of the species in the park, for example, is a massive undertaking requiring thousands of workers. In 2012, volunteers convened in RMNP for a 24-hour BioBlitz. From noon one day until noon the next, nearly 200 scientists and 5,000 volunteers counted all the living things they saw in RMNP. Their survey identified several species that had not been previously found in the park.

Thousands of Species

The official RMNP species list shows more than 3,200 species, including 278 kinds of birds, 676 types of insects, and more than

Citizen scientists monitor levels of mercury in the environment with the help of dragonfly larvae.

Other volunteers help conduct long-term studies. In one program, high school students gather samples of dragonfly larvae to study mercury. Mercury is a hazardous water contaminant that, like nitrogen, enters lakes in wild areas through air pollution. Scientists in RMNP joined a nationwide project that studies dragonflies to investigate levels of mercury. More than 3,000 volunteers in 90 parks have contributed to the overall study.

dragonfly larvae samples

dragonfly larvae

Thousands of Volunteers

Each year about 100 scientific research projects are conducted in RMNP. About 150 permanent employees, 200 seasonal employees, and more than 2,000 volunteers work in the park.

Citizen scientists monitor levels of mercury in the environment with the help of dragonfly larvae.

Why dragonflies? Because dragonfly larvae spend years living in the water before becoming adults. So, mercury levels in the larvae show whether there is mercury contamination in the water. In RMNP, students from the nearby Eagle Rock School and Professional Development Center scoop up dragonfly larvae to send to labs. There, the larvae are analyzed for mercury levels. The data are posted online, allowing people to compare results from different sites. In RMNP and elsewhere, citizen scientists make important contributions to scientific knowledge.

Volunteers work with NPS employees to identify and count specimens.

This quadrat square marks a small sample area of habitat. Scientists observe and record the number of each type of plant and animal within the square.

"*As individuals, we cannot control many things that will affect the park's future. Therefore, we must inform ourselves so that we can better address those things we can influence to preserve our beloved Rocky Mountain National Park.*"

— Thomas Gootz, Ph.D., author of *Transformation in Rocky Mountain National Park*

These citizen scientists are collecting samples in RMNP.

QUADRAT SAMPLING

Scientists studying ecosystems often want to know the populations of different animals and plants in an area. It's usually not practical to count each specimen individually, so scientists use sampling techniques, including *quadrat* sampling. You can try quadrat sampling in your yard, schoolyard, or park.

Supplies

- long tape measure
- 4 straight sticks, pencils, or fist-sized rocks
- about 10 feet (3 meters) of string or yarn
- a small notebook and a pen or pencil to take notes

Directions:

1. Locate a large outdoor area where plants are growing. This could be a field, garden, lawn, or backyard.

2. Choose a spot at random and measure out a square quadrat on the ground, 2 feet by 2 feet square (61 centimeters by 61 centimeters). Mark the four corners of the quadrat with rocks, or by poking a stick or pencil into the dirt in each corner.

3. Tie a string to each corner marker to mark the boundaries of your quadrat.

4. Examine the plants and animals within your square, and note your findings. How many species can you identify of plants, insects, and other living things? If you don't know their names, sketch what they look like. Can you count the individuals within the square?

5. For a scientific survey, you would examine several quadrats, record your results, and then estimate the populations of plant and animal species in the larger area using those results.

Glossary

adaptive (uh-DAP-tiv): changing or able to change in reaction to different circumstances

civilizations (siv-uh-li-ZAY-shuhnz): organized human societies

climate (KLYE-mit): the pattern of weather in a certain place over a long period of time

compounds (KAHM-poundz): substances, such as water or sugar, which are formed from two or more chemical elements like hydrogen or sodium

deposition (dep-uh-ZISH-uhn): the placing of a substance into a different location, as when nitrogen is moved out of the air and into the water and soil

exterminated (ik-STUR-muh-nate-id): destroyed or killed in large numbers

fertilizer (FUR-tuh-lye-zur): a substance added to soil or plants to make plants grow better

inventory (IN-vuhn-tor-ee): a complete list of items such as all that someone owns, or species in an area

microscopic (mye-kruh-SKAH-pik): visible only with a microscope; very tiny

policies (PAH-li-seez): general plans or rules that people follow when taking action or making decisions, as in government policies

sufficient (suh-FISH-uhnt): enough; as much as needed

tolerate (TAH-luh-rate): to continue to exist in difficult conditions

Index

Show What You Know

1. How do beavers change their environment?

2. What is the effect of excess nitrogen in environments that are naturally low in nitrogen?

3. How has climate change affected some of the plants and animals in Rocky Mountain National Park?

4. What is "ice patch archaeology"?

5. How can volunteers contribute to scientific research in Rocky Mountain National Park?

Further Reading

Carson, Mary Kay, *Park Scientists: Gila Monsters, Geysers, and Grizzly Bears in America's Own Backyard*, HMH Books for Young Readers, 2014.

Herman, Gail, *What is Climate Change?*, Penguin Workshop, 2018.

Zeiger, Jennifer, *Rocky Mountain*, Children's Press, 2018.

About the Author

Christy Mihaly is the author of kids' science books about topics including moose, redwood forests, elephants, and entomophagy—that's eating insects! She has explored national parks across the country, and helped create the Junior Ranger Activity Book published by National Geographic Kids in 2016. Her academic degrees are in environmental studies, policy studies, and law. She writes in Vermont under the supervision of her dog and cat. Find out more or say hello at her website: www.christymihaly.com.

www.rourkeeducationalmedia.com

PHOTO CREDITS: Cover foreground photo Courtesy Rocky Mountain National Park, cover bkground photo and title page © Chen.Z—Shutterstock.com, card with paper clip art © beths—Shutterstock.com; contents page National Park Service Photo/Todd M. Edgar, NPS; PAGE 4-5: RobertWaltman, haveseen, National Park Service; PAGE 6-7: C.Lopetz, Karsten_1, Matt Dirksen, Pavel Tvrd; PAGE 8-9: Jevtic, gnagel, eannetteKatzir; PAGE 10-11: Chase Dekke, Clopetz; PAGE 12-13: Jillian Cooper, CLopetz, marekuliasz; PAGE 14-15: National Park Service Photo/Todd M. Edgar, NPS, riekephotos, kavram, USGS-NWHC, elk fence photo C.Lopetz; PAGE 16-17: Jill Baron, USGS, US Forest service; PAGE 18-19: AlisLuch, grebeshkovmaxim, tupungato; PAGE 20-21: www.istock-editorial- Arina P. Habich, dschnarrs, aroon phadee; PAGE 22-23: USGS, Jevtic; PAGE 24-25: SeanXu, Schaef1, haveseen, Sparty1711, Greg westbrook; PAGE 26-27: randimal, Marina_Poushkina, Bruce Raynor, PhilAugustavo, talipcubukcu; PAGE 28-29: Kerry Hargrove, Fischer0182IDreamstime.com; PAGE 30-31: Bill Battaglin/ USGS Water Resources Division-Denver Federal Center, Forrest Brem- Creative Commons Attribution 2.5 Generic license; PAGE 32-33: National Park Service_pd, Nikolay_Voronin, Gift of William E. Weiss -PD, Images by Dr. Alan Lipkin; PAGE 34-35: National Park Service, John C. H. Grabill (LoC), Jose Gil; PAGE 36-37: National Park Service, Michael Murphy- Creative Commons Attribution 2.0 Generic, Aprilflower7-Creative Commons Attribution 2.0 Generic; PAGE 38-39: Photo by Sarah Diers (PolarTREC 2009/2010), Courtesy of ARCUS, National Park Service; PAGE 40-41: National Park Service Photo / Courtney Allen. NPS Photo/Todd M. Edgar, NPS Photo/Courtney Allen; PAGE 42-43: danlogan, VitalisG, National Park Service photo, NPS Photo/Todd M. Edgar; PAGE 44-45: National Park Service Photo_pd.

Edited by: Keli Sipperley

Produced by Blue Door Education for Rourke Educational Media. Cover design by: Nicola Stratford; Interior design and layout by: Jennifer Dydyk

Rocky Mountain / Christy Mihaly
(Natural Laboratories: Scientists in National Parks)
ISBN 978-1-64369-022-3 (hard cover)
ISBN 978-1-64369-116-9 (soft cover)
ISBN 978-1-64369-169-5 (e-Book)
Library of Congress Control Number: 2018956027

Printed in the United States of America, North Mankato, Minnesota